Leaping Towards the Extraordinary

One Family's Unconventional Journey Through Schooling and Travel

MEGAN SCHILLER

Netherstoned Press

Copyright © 2022 by Megan Schiller

All rights reserved. No portion of this book may be reproduced in any form without permission from the publisher, except as permitted by U.S. copyright law.

Grateful acknowledgment is made to Pilgrim for permission to reprint the chorus to the single, Chase Down the Moon, © 2017 by Pilgrim Records

This is a work of creative nonfiction. All of the events in this memoir are true to the best of the author's memory. Some names and identifying features have been changed to protect the identity of certain parties. The author in no way represents any company, corporation, or brand, mentioned herein. The views expressed in this memoir are solely those of the author.

Netherstoned Press

www.MeganSchiller.com

ISBN: 978-0-578-39959-1

For Karuna, Ora, and Aaron—who inspired me to leap, twirl, and shimmy and who bravely joined in to bust a move.

Contents

Limitless

PART 1 — 1

1. Oh Shit, I Forgot // *Mill Valley, California* — 3
2. Carpe Diem — 17
3. A Dose of Daring — 25
4. The Best Library in the World — 33
5. Planting Seeds — 37
6. Testing Truancy — 41
7. Setting a Date — 45
8. Falling into Place — 51
9. Unschooling — 57
10. Failed Experiments — 67
11. Official Start of Homeschool — 81
12. But First, Deschooling — 93
13. Making Our Work *Work* — 101

14. To Kindle the Fire	117
15. Election	123
16. The Cozy Comfort of Deschooling	127
17. In Search of School and Freedom	133
18. We Did It	141

PART 2

161

19. Our New Home // *Ohio*	163
20. Settling In // *Kentucky*	169
21. In Nashville, Every Party Turns Into a Music Jam // *Tennessee*	173
22. Our First Event // *North Carolina*	181
23. Roadschooling // *South Carolina*	191
24. A Birthday with Alligators // *Georgia*	199
25. Another Birthday in the Bayou // *Florida*	203
26. The Generosity of Strangers // *Louisiana*	209
27. Blindfolds and Family Canvases // *Texas*	213

28. The House of Eternal Return // *Oklahoma & New Mexico*	221
29. Two Auras, a Vortex, and a Premonition // *Arizona*	229
30. Creating Community // *California*	237
31. Beneath the Red Rocks // *Nevada & Utah*	243
32. But It's Nearly Summer! // *Colorado*	249
33. Pineapple Salsa // *Nebraska & Iowa*	257
34. Our Final Event and Live TV // *Illinois & Indiana*	261
35. Alumapalooza // *Ohio*	271
36. Full Circle // *Mill Valley, California*	279
37. Total Eclipse of the Heart // Idaho	287
Resources and Media Mentioned	295
Acknowledgments	299
About the Author	303

Life is either a daring adventure, or nothing.

—Helen Keller

Limitless

There's a beauty to the unexpected combination of our family of four being contained in this cramped and tiny home—a mere 175 square feet—yet feeling more freedom than I've ever known. With only a few possessions and the flexibility to move our home when and where we want, life feels limitless. Our living space expands well beyond these aluminum walls, into dense forests and across white sands. Our community grows with each stop, each campsite. New friends ask us to dinner, and we tell stories around campfires to welcoming neighbors who invite us to roast marshmallows. And although we often sleep by a quiet lake or under knowing trees, it doesn't really matter where we end up each night. Whether in a crowded RV park or a barren asphalt lot, we have our home. We're together as a family, learning to appreciate these cozy quarters, learning to truly live our lives. This isn't a vacation, and we aren't trying to hit all the tourist sights. We are working, living, and schooling on the road—and it's extraordinary.

hips and chatting about kids and daily life. Ora ran off to the play structure, and I headed towards Karuna's classroom.

One mom waved hello from a cluster and I waved back, unsure whether to stop and join in the conversation or keep walking. I slowed down and popped into the crowd, eager to have an adult conversation after a day of three-year-old banter. But as the chatting resumed, I stood there, awkwardly waiting for the right moment to add something to the discussion. When a few minutes passed and nothing came out of my mouth, I quickly announced, "Gotta go get Karuna!" and ducked out from the group towards the second grade.

Karuna was outside her classroom, backpack on, and whispering with a new friend, Melissa, as I approached.

"Hi, sweetie!" I said as she moved towards me. She waved goodbye to Melissa and began walking with me to get Ora from the play structure. "How was school?" I asked.

"Boring," she moaned. "And the librarian didn't let me get the book I wanted."

"Why not?"

"She said it was above my grade level."

"Well that's odd," I mumbled. Then I wondered, *Even if it was meant for an older audience, it was in an elementary school library, how inappropriate could it be? And if it was merely a policy to keep kids reading at their skill level, isn't it more likely that children will improve their reading skills if the material is of interest?*

When we got home, I made some snacks for the girls and Karuna quietly retreated to the hanging hammock chair in her bedroom with a graphic novel in hand. Before second grade, Karuna spent most of her free time doing art and playing pretend with Ora. They would play "sisters" and other imaginative games with toys and props. By second grade, Karuna was only interested in being with friends, reading graphic novels, playing Minecraft, and occasionally drawing. Was this just part of growing up? Were her interests changing? Sometimes it felt like she was a disgruntled pre-teen, and I had to remind myself that she was only seven years old!

One afternoon that same October, our friend Colin stopped by to say hello. He left us with a documentary called *Class Dismissed* and encouraged us to watch it. It documented a family in Southern California as they pulled their two kids out of middle school and explored various styles of homeschooling. Neither Aaron nor I had any interest in homeschooling, so it ended up sitting on the cabinet next to our TV for a few weeks, waiting patiently to reveal its magic, like a hidden crystal geode inside a dull rock. Sometimes I wonder, if Colin hadn't thought to bring this movie over or if we had simply forgotten to watch it, would our lives be radically different today?

Weeks later I found myself looking around for the TV remote after the girls went to sleep. The DVD case caught my eye, so I picked it up and read the description on the back. Feeling a tiny twinge of curiosity, I slid the disk into the DVD player and called Aaron over to watch with me.

Ten minutes into the movie, I thought to myself, *Oh shit, I forgot.*

I'd forgotten what I believed in.

◎

It was the fall of 2015. My husband, Aaron, and I were living with our two daughters, Karuna and Ora in Mill Valley, a suburban town outside of San Francisco. By a miraculous turn of events, we ended up living in my grandmother's old cottage, now owned by my father, in a coveted neighborhood where the San Francisco tech and finance crowd moves to when they have kids.

I felt extremely lucky to be living there and was pretty content with the way our lives were unfolding, at least I thought I was. Looking back, I can see that there was no depth to that happiness. I wasn't deeply connected to our community, to Karuna's school, to the choices we were making about work and finances—but I had no idea of any of that at the time.

I had settled into our comfy suburban life and was simply going through the same motions as everyone else. My blog and business, *The Art Pantry*—a mix of kids' art education and interior design—was picking up with bigger client projects, and I was consistently updating my website and digital products. Aaron was in his second year of a local counseling program and in the early stages of his private coaching/counseling practice.

We had friends in our community, dozens of families, just like ours, sprinkled among the homes in our neighborhood. Families simply living their lives as best they could, doing the suburban thing, but under the surface what was brewing? I wasn't convinced that everything was exactly as it appeared. *There has to be more going on for everyone than what's visible from the surface, right? Will this really be my life for the next 15 years?* When I would do a school pick-up or go to a "moms' night out," I told myself I was enjoying the social connection and friendliness, but somewhere inside I always felt distant, like an outsider. The feeling reminded me of being back in junior high and vying for the attention of the cool girls.

I didn't even realize that I felt this way at the time. I had shut off my connection to my deeper emotions and awareness, and I assumed my experience was just a natural outcome of my reserved nature. The neighborhood moms would often meet for a "moms' night out" dinner at one of the fancy restaurants in town. I would eat at home first and then join them for a drink without mentioning that I simply couldn't afford to eat there. During dinner, most of them were chatting wildly around me, and I would chime in here and there without having much to say.

I felt incredibly out of place but didn't allow myself to entertain the idea that I shouldn't be there. *These are my friends!* These were the women who raised kids with me, who brought their kids to my art classes, who shared their front yards on lazy afternoons while we nursed babies and talked about parenting. But as the kids grew older and there was no longer a need to swap stories of sleep training, I began to notice that the conversations became less and less relevant to my life. And eventually I just stopped contributing much to the conversations.

So, when I sat down to watch the documentary for the first time, I felt a whisper, a tugging at my soul, that I hadn't felt in a long time. It was reminding me of what I believed about kids and learning—what I connected with in high school when I read *The Teenage Liberation Handbook: How to Quit School and Get a Real Life and Education*.

When had I forgotten? Maybe once I left the confines of high school and was finally in control of my own education, it slipped from the edges of my memories. Maybe it was when I fell in love with teaching preschool and discovered the expansiveness of child-led learning and the Reggio Emilia approach to early childhood education. I was so engrossed in the freedom of this preschool philosophy that I began to welcome the institution of school again. I forgot what happens in the years that follow. I forgot that a good public school still does not equal child-led learning and freedom.

Maybe I got caught up in the allure of our affluent community and thought that the private money being poured into our public school was good enough. Or maybe I was wooed by the three-block walk to school and the promise of our children's lives safely contained in this small town.

But even beyond all that, this documentary reminded me that I wasn't living life by my values and that I had lost my ambition for the extraordinary. It whispered that I had slipped unknowingly onto a safe and easy path and had forgotten this truth that I'd known when I was younger: *life is meant to be extraordinary.* It is meant to be deeply joyful, amazing, and exciting. If we aren't actively moving towards the extraordinary or seeing the extraordinary within our everyday lives, then what's the point?

This spark—this epiphany—hit me like a hummingbird diving for nectar. It happened in a flash. I could see the beauty and possibility in front of me, but I had to approach slowly so as not to scare it away. I wasn't going to do anything rash, like yank Karuna out of her second grade class and immediately jump into this dazzling unknown. I wanted to take my time, to understand Karuna's perspective, to ease the family into flight.

⋒

For the next few weeks, I continued to feel these nudges, like a bony elbow pressing firmly into my back and inching me off the paved road. It was pushing me towards a dirt path that appeared wild and exciting, but held the possibility of isolation and regret.

The more I sat with this curiosity, the more conflicted I became. On my way to pick up Ora from preschool, I would often stop by a small trail along Richardson Bay and sit on a bench to try to work out my emotions. I knew Ora's time at her Reggio-inspired preschool was spent playing and exploring. I knew she had plenty of time outside, pouring water down the dirt hill, building with large wooden blocks, playing pretend with friends, climbing, collecting twigs and leaves in the eucalyptus grove. Ora's daily school experience was one of wonder and joy. I couldn't say the same for Karuna.

I would often feel an aching in my gut when I thought of Karuna at school, being herded in and out of the classroom at the sound of a bell. Sitting at a desk for hours, filling out worksheets, while the joy of learning was quickly being sucked out of her soul. It reminded me of a painting I made in high school of a girl, swirling with color, head bent in despair, body curled up behind bars. *So dramatic*, I know, but I was 16 and it was also kind of true.

Then I would imagine having Karuna with me on the trail, walking along the bay, climbing trees and collecting shells, wondering about the world around us. The things that she was studying in science were here with me on the edge of the bay, not in her classroom. The language and literature of her second grade curriculum weren't really in the classroom either. They were in the voices of our community, they were in the public library, in the books that might be above her grade level, yet inspired her to want to read.

The "urban environments" she was learning about in social studies weren't on the pages of her textbook; they were across the Golden Gate Bridge on the streets of San Francisco. They were in Oakland, where we visited often to see my parents and sister. And they were in the boroughs of New York where we would spend a week during winter break to visit my brother and his family. The more I thought about how confining this classroom was, the more I felt compelled to liberate her.

When talking about school with Karuna, it dawned on me that she had begun to understand a sad and telling equation: Learning = School. School sucks; therefore, learning sucks. School is boring; therefore, learning is boring.

What was happening to her? *If this is what second grade is like, what happens after a few more years of this? Do I want her to go through life accepting that school is boring and that's just the way it goes until she gets to college and is able to finally choose for herself what she wants to do? By then she'll be so out of touch with her own curiosity and thirst for knowledge that she'll have to unlearn everything in order to appreciate learning again.*

I wasn't sure about her social scene either. I would pay attention to her mood after school or playdates. Some of the new friends she was making were rubbing off on her in a way that didn't feel right to me.

One day Karuna came home from school and I asked her how her day was. She casually mentioned that Melissa was sitting on the side of the playground and quietly making fun of kids' fashion choices as they passed by. I didn't know Melissa at all, so I asked more about her and what kinds of things they do at school together. It turned out that Melissa also liked to play tricks on some of the kindergarteners and then laugh at them when they were confused. Karuna could see how this was not very kind behavior, but she brushed it off and still seemed to enjoy hanging out with Melissa. Teasing, gossiping, and bullying can be common experiences in school, even in second grade, but they don't *have* to be. And it wasn't okay with me. It was just one more nudge that was telling me to *get Karuna out of there*.

I let this awakening sink in while I began to search for clues. *What's next? What do I do with this feeling now that it's here?* I knew that what I was feeling was not just about education and our kids—it was so much bigger than that. I also sensed that change begins with curiosity and that this spark was worth following. I began to consume as much information as I could on homeschooling and "unschooling." I was terrified of walking down this road, and yet it felt more exciting and soul-rejuvenating than anything I had felt in a long time. To pacify the fear, I decided to write out a pro-and-con list for homeschooling.

Pros:
Aligns with values
Will be an incredible experience for our family
Will give the girls an amazing education
Will create strong bonds between us
Will help keep social experiences positive
Allows for adventures and flexibility

Cons:
If we leave, we have to give up our spot at Evergreen School
Potentially ostracized by our community
Potential confusion and lack of support from our extended family
We lose our daily babysitter (school)

One list is exciting, full of hope and *joie de vivre*. The other is heavy and full of fear. I asked myself, *Which one is the life I want to live?*

2

Carpe Diem

Adventure and intuition have always been a part of me. Growing up in the hills of Oakland, California, in the '80s was an experience of simultaneous urban grit and a quiet life in the woods. Our home was on a double lot, high in the hills, surrounded by eucalyptus, bay, and redwood trees with blackberry bushes pouring out of the open spaces. When I was three years old and my brother, Scott, was five, our dad built us a treehouse—which was basically my second home, with an actual staircase leading up to the door. I spent much of my childhood out there in the treehouse or roaming the property with clippers, foraging on edible leaves and fruit.

Our parents held the belief that aside from the necessities and unconditional parental love, children should raise themselves. We were free to wander the neighborhood and often discovered secret hideouts and wild woods to explore.

When I was about seven, my brother and his friend Michael, our neighbor down the road, let me in on a new frontier—the wilderness that rolled out from behind Michael's house in what seemed like acres of undeveloped land. We called it "Nettle Land" for the pesky prickly plants that dotted the landscape. They were stoic and protective, like guards of this kingdom, fighting off intruders with their stinging armor. We learned to navigate the nettles, and it became our favorite place to be. We'd build forts and become characters from *Star Wars* or *Indiana Jones*. Scott and Michael would often bring along a video camera and use Nettle Land as the location for their epic homemade movies—and by "epic," I mean precarious scenes shot on a shaky camcorder and strung together to resemble a plot.

This sort of woodsy adventuring continued into high school when we moved across town. We were on the other side of the Oakland hills, but this time further down the hill, closer to shops, schools, and freeways. Thankfully, I could still walk a block up my street and arrive at the opening of a hiking trail. It wrapped around the hill and pushed back into thick redwoods with a creek running through the middle. I didn't build forts anymore or play pretend, but this soon became my new favorite place to be. It was my thinking place, my writing place. I would ponder life's existential teenage questions, sitting on the edge of the hill, scanning over Oakland

and out to San Francisco. I began to bring friends to this trail, and we named it Narnia (from the enchanted land of *The Lion, the Witch, and the Wardrobe*). It was our connection to magic, to freedom.

⋒

When I was in the tenth grade, my mom found out that I had been smoking weed, and she confronted me in the car one afternoon. "But, Mom, it expands my mind!" I proclaimed. I went on to plead my case that my grades had actually improved due to this "mind expansion." She listened and acknowledged that, yes, my grades *had* improved.

"Just don't do it in the house." Her uneasy words sounded more like a plea than a command. "I don't want your friends to think that our house is the party house." I agreed. So when friends came over, we walked to Narnia and would smoke a bowl, looking out at the view or sitting by the creek, and philosophize about life.

Getting high was something that initially *was* expansive. I really meant what I said to my mom. For me it always equated with adventure and deep questions about life and God and the ways of the universe. When I started smoking weed, I also became intensely interested in learning, writing, and spirituality. It kicked on some part of my brain that had been dormant all through puberty, as I had been focused solely on social dynamics. But once weed entered my life I desperately wanted to read poetry and philosophy and get to some understanding about the meaning of life. I was also attending a Catholic high school, which in Oakland, was really just a way out of the public school system and a much less expensive route than a secular private school.

The majority of students in my school weren't Catholic, but we did have to take one religious studies class each semester, and we had the option of attending a monthly Mass. All of my friends chose study hall over Mass, but something was calling me to learn more. Although I was baptized and grew up going to midnight Mass on Christmas Eve, I didn't feel Catholic or Christian. I also had Jewish heritage on my dad's side but didn't feel connected to that either. What I felt was a deep curiosity for religion and a quest for answers about the ways of the universe. So I chose Mass over study hall and started reading religious texts to feed this curiosity.

In the tenth grade, the electives for religious studies broadened, and I took classes like World Religions and Living and Dying. In World Religions I learned about Buddhism, which enamored me with its teachings on suffering, compassion, and meditation. And as it turned out, the theme of the Living and Dying class was "Carpe diem: seize the day!" This seemingly random adage, "seize the day," nestled inside my soul and leaked whispers into my veins throughout my adolescence. Who knew that it would drift in and out of hibernation and then make an appearance two decades later as I stood on the porch looking out to our white picket fence? I have a feeling that my Living and Dying teacher, Father Malo, might have known. Maybe he planted that seed so that each of us, his captivated students, would move out into the world with his favorite lesson imprinted on our bones.

These adolescent insights were invigorating. I was hungry for understanding, for life, for adventure. I spent my weekends with friends smoking weed and trekking across Oakland and Berkeley on foot, open to unexpected discoveries along the way. After many months of this, the weed caught up with us. We stopped adventuring around and would instead opt to hang at one of our houses, draped over the bed or sofa, like Slinkies stuck in motion.

◫

A pivotal moment came one Saturday afternoon when I was in the eleventh grade. A few friends and I were sitting on the staircase in my front hallway. We were stoned and very sluggish. No one wanted to do anything. No one wanted to move from the staircase. I pleaded with them, "Come oooooon. Aren't you guys sick of sitting around all the time? What happened to us? What about our adventures? Let's dooooo something!"

They looked at me with glazed eyes and let out a little giggle. "Oh, Megan, you and your adventures." Their words were mixed with pity and a bit of surrender. Like I was chasing something too fast for us all and it was time to let it go. The weed had melted away our collective curiosity and exuberance.

It was then that I felt that intuitive nudge and knew it was time to say goodbye to my green companion and journey on without it. This also meant that I would be leaving behind my friends, these sisters, in an inevitable quest that I could no longer ignore.

After that, I was driven to follow that nudge. I stopped smoking weed, drinking alcohol, and going to parties. I spent my time reading travel adventures, writing poetry, and painting tortured images of a girl behind bars or caught in a snake's coil. I felt trapped in the conditions of my teenage life, and yet I instinctively knew I could choose a way out.

I averted the imprisonment of school by making it my own. I would skip school on days when I'd rather read at a coffee shop or walk along a wooded trail. But I also embraced education at its core and chose electives that enabled my curiosity. Remember, I was an avid reader of *The Teenage Liberation Handbook: How to Quit School and Get a Real Life and Education*. While I didn't quit school, I did whatever I could to explore the self-guided "unschooling" philosophy that the book encouraged. At school, I was a good student, quiet and submissive, so my tardies and absences were never questioned.

The more I pushed against social norms, the wider the chasm became between me and my friends. They were hurt and angry at me for walking away. They had forgotten that day on the stairs and my unwillingness to give in to the doldrums.

The summer after eleventh grade, I had already made plans with one of those friends to spend a month in the artsy colonial town of San Miguel de Allende, Mexico. We had been there together the summer before to study art and Spanish and it was life-changing. As we arrived this time, we both knew things were different between us. She confronted me right away and told me that I had hurt her with my distance. She wanted me to apologize and go back to the way things were. I was sorry I had caused her any pain. I never meant to hurt her. But also I felt strongly that I wasn't sorry for walking away. I wasn't sorry for following my intuition rather than following my friends, for choosing myself over what was expected of me, for choosing curiosity over numbness and partying. I told her this. I apologized for unintentionally hurting her, but I wasn't going to apologize for my actions. I told her that I wasn't sorry for that part and that I hoped she could understand my perspective.

That was the end of our friendship for the next year. She stopped speaking to me, completely baffled at how I could put my own needs before our sisterhood. We lived together for a month in Mexico in this way. Tiptoeing around each other. She was angry and disappointed. I was disappointed in the silence between us, but I also felt at peace. It wasn't the peace of harmony or reconciliation, it was the kind of peace that comes when you realize your actions are finally in alignment with your intuition. Any fear or doubt I had was overcome by a deep knowing that I was moving in the right direction.